Curvy Log Cabin Quilts

by Jean Ann Wright

Landauer Publishing

Curvy Log Cabin Quilts
by Jean Ann Wright

Landauer Publishing (*www.landauerpub.com*) is an imprint of
Fox Chapel Publishing Company, Inc.

Editor: Jeri Simon

Art Director: Laurel Albright

Photographer: Sue Voegtlin

ISBN: 978-1-935726-68-5

We are always looking for talented authors. To submit an idea,
please send a brief inquiry to acquisitions@foxchapelpublishing.com.

Printed in China
10 9 8 7 6 5

Table of Contents

Selecting Log Cabin Block Fabrics

Log cabin blocks are made using light and dark value fabrics for the logs, as well as a center square. The fabric logs are sewn around the center square until the desired size is achieved. When selecting fabrics for log cabin blocks it is important to determine whether you want a scrappy quilt using every "crayon" in the box or a

Log Cabin Block

Courthouse Steps Log Cabin Block

Half Log Cabin Block

carefully planned quilt with a limited fabric palette. The curvy log cabin block is used to create the illusion of curved designs with clear visual differences between the light and dark value fabric logs.

Choosing a Method

When making the curvy log cabin blocks, choose the cut-to-size or trim-to-size method and follow the lessons given on pages 6-11. All the quilts in this book can be made using either method.

Cut-to-size method

Traditionally, log cabin blocks were made with fabric logs cut-to-size. The measurements of the fabric logs were calculated to fit exactly around a center square. The time and attention given to precise cutting is the key to making log cabin blocks in the cut-to-size method.

Sewing a log cabin block using the cut-to-size method requires exact cutting of the center square and each of the fabric logs that will be used to make the block. Use the charts on pages 12-13 for measurements to make curvy log cabin blocks in different sizes.

Trim-to-size method

The Curvy Log Cabin Trim Tool utilizes a trim-to-size method. The center square is the only precision cut piece in the trim-to-size method.

Sewing a curvy log cabin block using the Curvy Log Cabin Trim Tool allows you to use fabric logs cut in any width. The fabric logs must be cut straight on one side but can be ripped or uneven on the other side. The Curvy Log Cabin Trim Tool is used to trim each round of logs to size before adding the next round. Although most log cabin quilts have three rounds of logs around the center square, you can add as few or as many rounds as you wish.

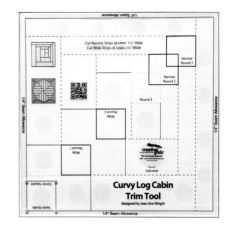

Sewing Tips

- The log cabin block is made entirely of straight seams sewn with a scant 1/4" seam allowance. Keeping seam allowances consistent in size is very important. If the seam allowances vary in width the finished blocks will vary in size as well.

- Chain piecing a series of blocks is a speed technique that can be used when making cut-to-size blocks and trim-to-size blocks.

- Fabric logs are sewn in a clockwise direction around a center square. It is not necessary to pin the logs in place before sewing. If you wish to pin, simply place a pin at the bottom of each strip along the outside edge to hold the log in place. Pinning guards against fabric shifting as it moves through the feed dogs.

- Always position the log you are adding on the top of the pieces you have already sewn, right sides together. This helps maintain a consistent size for each completed block when using the cut-to-size method.

- Finger press the seams after each log is added and before adding the next log to your block. When a complete round of four logs is sewn to the center square, press with an iron. Using a spray starch or fabric sizing during the final pressing adds body to the completed block.

Curvy Log Cabin

The curvy log cabin block starts with a precision cut center square. Wide and narrow fabric logs are then added in a clockwise rotation to make rounds around the square. Each round consists of two wide and two narrow logs. The block is started with the wide logs. Press away from the center square as you add each log.

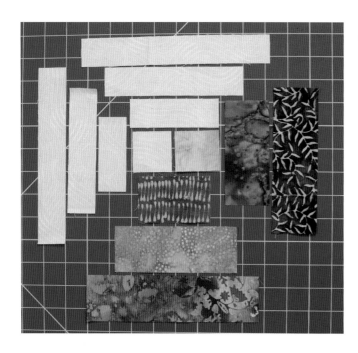

1 Determine the size of the log cabin block you wish to make and use the chart on page 13 to cut the center square and logs to the required size.

We are making an 8" finished block in our example so our center square is 1-3/4".

Tip: You may wish to number the logs as you cut them.

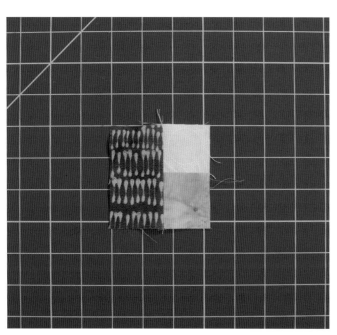

2 Sew wide logs #1 and #2 to adjacent sides of the center square in a clockwise rotation.

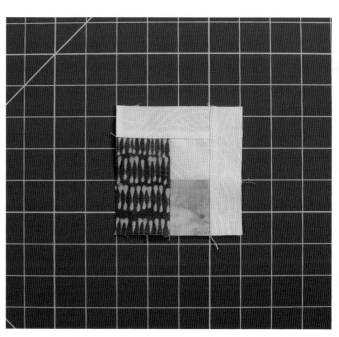

3 Sew narrow logs #3 and #4 to the two remaining adjacent sides of the center square continuing in a clockwise rotation. This completes round #1.

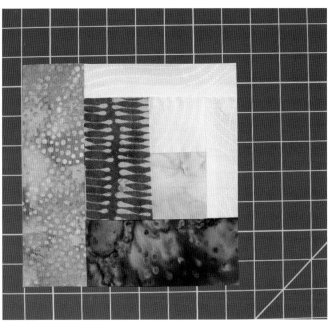

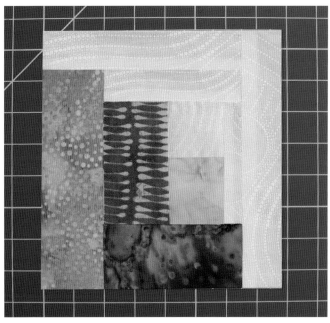

4 Sew wide logs #5 and #6 to adjacent sides of round #1 in a clockwise rotation.

5 Sew narrow logs #7 and #8 to the two remaining adjacent sides of round #1 continuing in a clockwise rotation. This completes round #2.

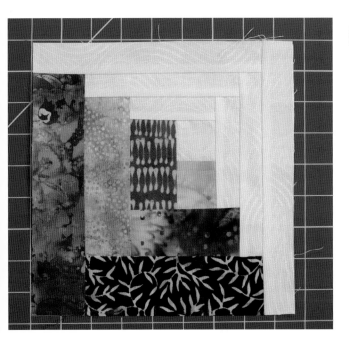

6 Sew two wide (#9, #10) and two narrow (#11, #12) logs in a clockwise rotation to round #2 to complete the curvy log cabin block. Press using spray starch or fabric stabilizer.

Making Blocks Using the Curvy Log Cabin Trim Tool

The Curvy Log Cabin Trim Tool is a quick and easy way to make perfect blocks every time. Only one side of the fabric log needs to be rotary cut and the logs do not need to be cut to size. The other side of the log can be ripped, angled or wavy, as the logs in each round will be trimmed to size after being sewn in place. Using the Trim Tool eliminates time spent cutting each log to size so you can start with the fun part—sewing the blocks.

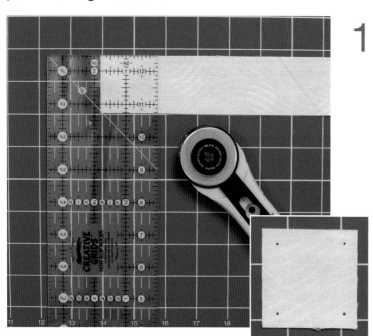

1 Cut precise 1-3/4" squares for the center of each 8" log cabin block. Rotary cut one side of the fabric logs so you have a straight edge. The wide logs need to be cut at least 2-1/4" wide and the narrow logs at least 1-1/2" wide.

Note: The Trim Tool's center square seam guide may be used to mark the seam allowance on the wrong side of the center square. It is not necessary, but may help in precisely sewing the first round of logs to the center square.

2 With right sides together, line up the rotary cut edge of a wide log on one side of a center square. Stitch along the edge using a scant 1/4" seam allowance.

Snip the log slightly longer than the center square. Finger press the seam toward the log.

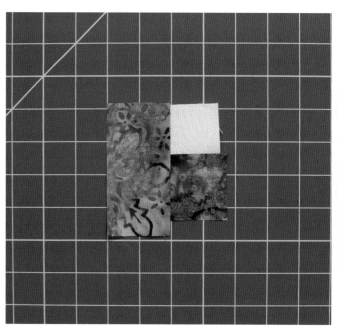

3 With right sides together, align the rotary cut edge of another wide log on the adjacent side of the center square, overlapping the previously added log. Stitch along the edge using a scant 1/4" seam allowance. Finger press the seam toward the log.

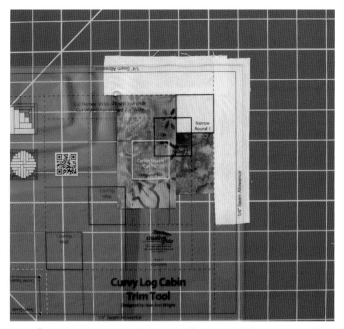
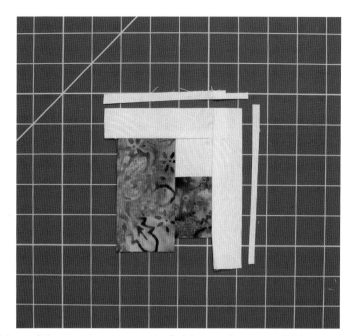

4 Sew two narrow logs on the remaining two adjacent sides of the center square to finish sewing round #1. Press with an iron.

Position the Narrow Round 1 square on the Trim Tool on the center square. Trim the two narrow sides along the right and upper edges of the Trim Tool as shown.

Tip: Line up the dotted lines on the Trim Tool with the seam lines of the block before trimming.

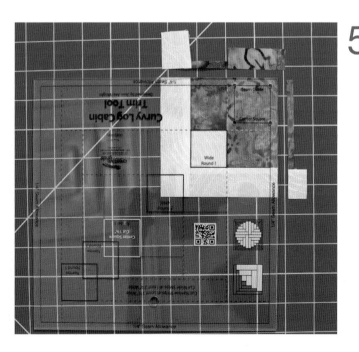

5 Turn the block 180-degrees and position the Wide Round 1 square on the Trim Tool on the center square. Trim the two wide sides along the right and upper edges of the Trim Tool as shown to complete round #1.

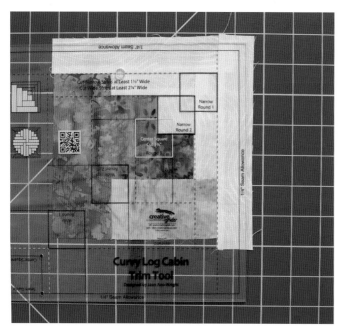
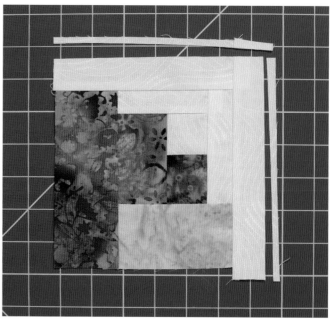

6 Referring to steps 2-4, sew two wide logs to adjacent sides of the block, aligning them with the wide logs from round #1. Sew the narrow logs on the remaining two adjacent sides of the block aligning them with the narrow logs from round #1. Press with an iron.

Position the Narrow Round 2 square on the Trim Tool on the center square as shown and trim the narrow sides along the right and upper edges of the Trim Tool.

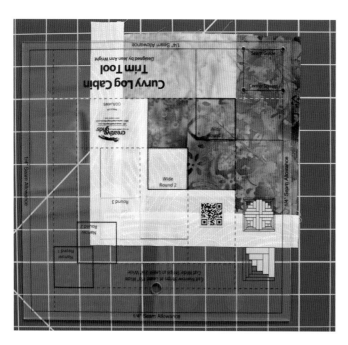

7 Turn the block 180-degrees and position the Wide Round 2 square on the Trim Tool on the center square as shown. Trim the two wide sides along the right and upper edges of the Trim Tool to complete round #2.

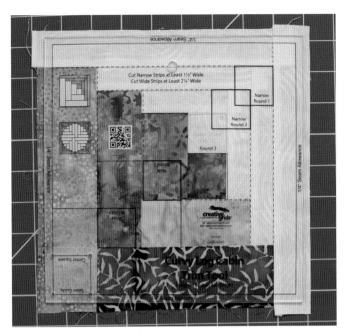

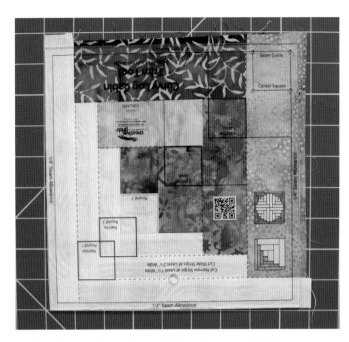

8 Referring to steps 2-4, sew two wide logs and two narrow logs in a clockwise rotation to round #2 to complete the curvy log cabin block. Press with an iron.

Position the Center Square Round 3 on the Trim Tool on the center square of the block as shown.

9 Trim all four sides beginning with the two narrow sides. When turning the block to trim, keep the Trim Tool and block aligned.

Learn to use the Curvy Log Cabin Trim Tool

Curvy Log Cabin Trim Tool Yardage Chart

The fabric calculations given are for cutting strips with the 6" and 8" Curvy Log Cabin Trim Tools. A slightly larger amount of strips from each fat quarter will occur if you are cutting your strips to exact size using the charts on page 13.

6" Finished Block A

Cut size		Finished size
Center Square: 1½"		Center square: scant 1"
Narrow Logs: 1¼"		Narrow Logs: ⅝"
Wide Logs: 1¾"		Wide Logs: 1⅛"

For 7 Blocks	Yardage	Cutting
Center Square	narrow log fabric	cut (7) 1½" squares
Narrow Logs	fat ¼ or ¼ yard	yields strips for 7 blocks
Wide Logs	fat ¼ or ¼ yard	yields strips for 7 blocks

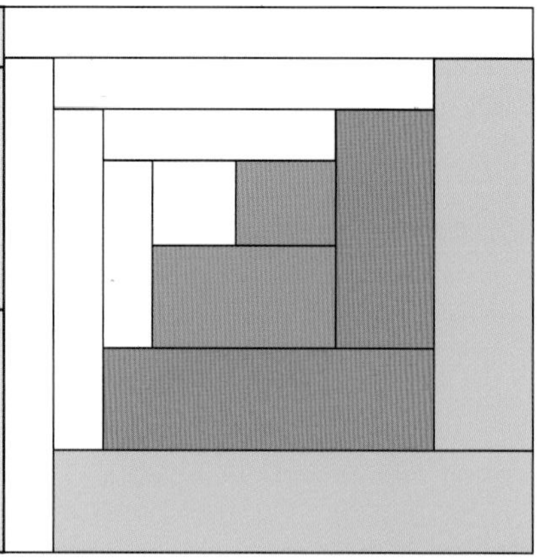

6" Finished Block B

Cut size		Finished size
Center square: 1½"		Center square: scant 1"
Narrow Logs: 1¼"		Narrow Logs: ⅝"
Wide Logs: 1¾"		Wide Logs: 1⅛"

For 11/6 Blocks	Yardage	Cutting
Center Square	narrow log fabric	cut (6) 1½" squares
Narrow Logs	fat ¼ or ¼ yard	yields strips for 11 blocks
Wide Logs	fat ¼ or ¼ yard	yields strips for 6 blocks

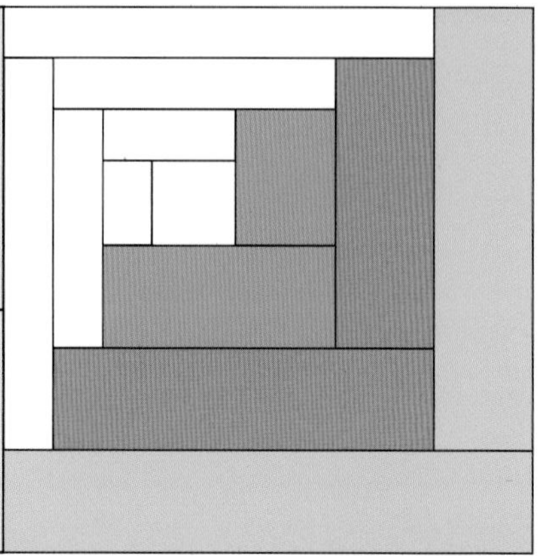

8" Finished Block A

Cut size		Finished size
Center square: 1¾"		Center square: 1¼"
Narrow Logs: 1½"		Narrow Logs: ¾"
Wide Logs: 2¼"		Wide Logs: 1½"

For 5 Blocks	Yardage	Cutting
Center Square	narrow log fabric	cut (5) 1¾" squares
Narrow Logs	fat ¼ or ¼ yard	yields strips for 5 blocks
Wide Logs	fat ¼ or ¼ yard	yields strips for 5 blocks

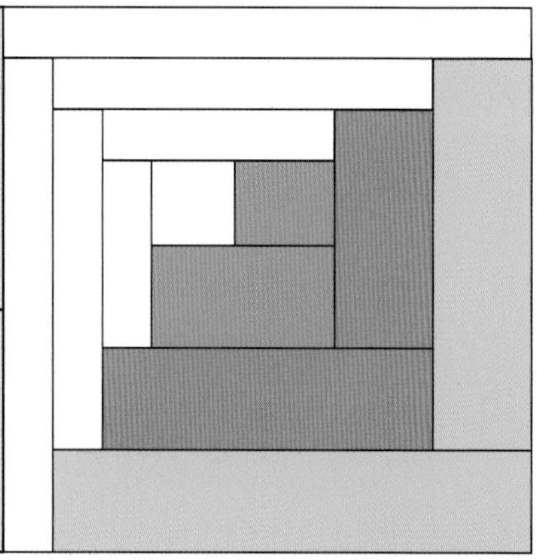

8" Finished Block B

Cut size		Finished size
Center square: 1¾"		Center square: 1¼"
Narrow Logs: 1½"		Narrow Logs: ¾"
Wide Logs: 2¼"		Wide Logs: 1½"

For 7/4 Blocks	Yardage	Cutting
Center Square	narrow log fabric	cut (4) 1¾" squares
Narrow Logs	fat ¼ or ¼ yard	yields strips for 7 blocks
Wide Logs	fat ¼ or ¼ yard	yields strips for 4 blocks

Cut-to-Size Diagram for 6" Curvy Log Cabin Block A

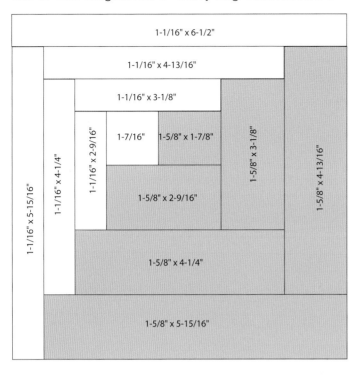

Cut-to-Size Diagram for 6" Curvy Log Cabin Block B

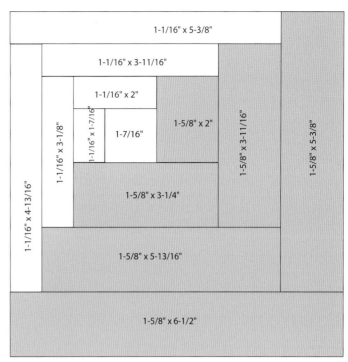

Cut-to-Size Diagram for 8" Curvy Log Cabin Block A

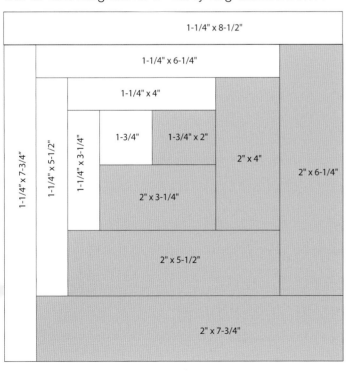

Cut-to-Size Diagram for 8" Curvy Log Cabin Block B

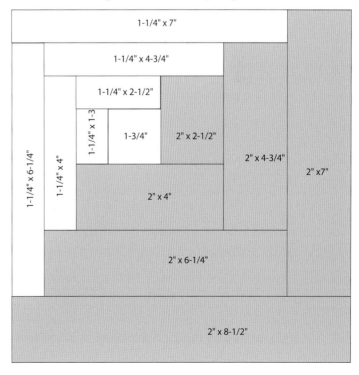

13

Solomon's Puzzle Quilt

The popular Drunkard's Path block, also known as Solomon's Puzzle, inspired the blocks for this quilt. Each block unit is made with sixteen curvy log cabin blocks. Rich hues in bright batiks combine with royal reds and golds to celebrate King Solomon known for his wisdom and ability to solve difficult puzzles.

Skill level: intermediate
Finished quilt size: 64" x 64"
Curvy log cabin block size: 6" x 6"
48 Block A1; 16 Block A2
wof indicates width of fabric
wofq indicates width of fat quarter

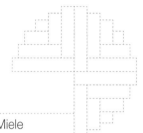

Quilt designed and pieced by Jean Ann Wright; quilted by Alta Miele

Fabric Requirements

- 18 assorted bright batik fat quarters for blocks

Note: The featured quilt uses aqua, green, gold, red, purple and royal blue. You may also use batik scraps.

- 2-1/2 yards white fabric for blocks

- 1/2 yard gold fabric for block unit borders and sashing square

- 1-3/4 yards red orange fabric for sashing, outer border and binding

- 4-3/4 yards backing fabric

Cutting

Note: Refer to the Cutting Diagrams for 6" blocks on page 13 to cut the fabric logs to size. The block cutting directions given are for using the Curvy Log Cabin Trim Tool. The trim tool fabric logs must be cut at least 1-1/4" and 1-3/4" wide to allow for trimming.

From assorted bright batik fat quarters, cut:

(48) 1-1/2" center squares for Block A1.

(60) 1-1/4" x wofq strips for Block A1.

(32) 1-3/4" x wofq strips for Block A2.

Note: Reserve any leftover fat quarter fabric to cut more strips if necessary.

From white fabric, cut:

(16) 1-1/2" center squares for Block A2.

(30) 1-3/4" x wof strips for Block A1.

(16) 1-1/4" x wof strips for Block A2.

Note: Reserve any white fabric to cut more strips if necessary.

From gold fabric, cut:

(1) 2-1/2" sashing square.

(12) 1-1/2" x wof strips. Sew strips together end-to-end and cut:
- (8) 1-1/2" x 24-1/2" block unit border strips and
- (8) 1-1/2" x 26-1/2" block unit border strips.

From red orange fabric, cut:

(3) 2-1/2" x wof strips. Sew strips together end-to-end and cut:
- (4) 2-1/2" x 26-1/2" sashing strips.

(6) 5-1/2" x wof strips. Sew strips together end-to-end and cut:
- (2) 5-1/2" x 54-1/2" side borders and
- (2) 5-1/2" x 64-1/2" top/bottom borders.

(7) 2-1/4" x wof binding strips.

Block Assembly

Note: Refer to pages 6-11 to sew the blocks together using your preferred method. Sewing sequence diagrams are provided on pages 12-13 to assist in adding the strips in the correct direction and order.

Block A1

1. Sew (2) wide white strips to adjacent sides of a batik center square in a clockwise rotation. Sew (2) narrow batik strips to the remaining sides of the center square continuing in a clockwise rotation. This completes round #1. Press the completed round. If you are using the Curvy Log Cabin Trim Tool, trim round #1 to size.

2. Refer to step 1 to add rounds #2 and #3 to the block. Press and trim the logs after each round is complete. Make 48 block A1.

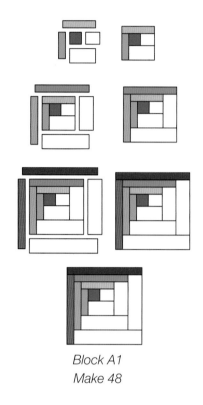

Block A1
Make 48

Block A2

1. Sew (2) wide batik strips to adjacent sides of a white center square in a clockwise rotation. Sew (2) narrow white strips to the remaining sides of the center square continuing in a clockwise rotation. This completes round #1. Press the completed round. If you are using the Curvy Log Cabin Trim Tool, trim round #1 to size.

2. Refer to step 1 to add rounds #2 and #3 to the block. Press and trim the logs after each round is complete. Make 16 block A2.

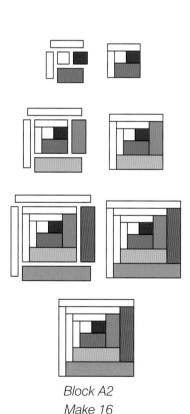

Block A2
Make 16

Block Unit Assembly

1. Lay out 3 block A1 and 1 block A2 in 4 rows with 4 blocks in each row as shown.

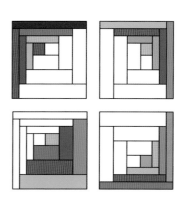

2. Sew the blocks together in rows.

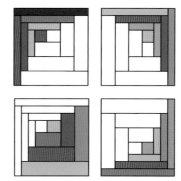

3. Sew the rows together to make a block unit. Make 16 block units.

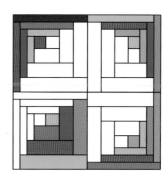

Make 16

4. Lay out 4 block units in 2 rows with 2 units in each row. Sew the units together to make a quadrant. Make 4 quadrants.

Make 4

5. Sew a 1-1/2" x 24-1/2" gold block unit border strip to opposite sides of a quadrant. Sew a 1-1/2" x 26-1/2" gold block unit border strip to the top/bottom of the quadrant. Press seams toward the borders. Repeat with the remaining quadrants.

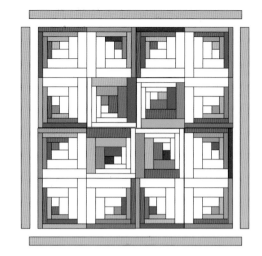

Quilt Assembly

1. Lay out 4 quadrants, (4) 2-1/2" x 26-1/2" red orange sashing strips and a 2-1/2" gold sashing square in 3 rows as shown in the Quilt Assembly Diagram.

2. Sew the pieces together in rows. Sew the rows together to complete the quilt center.

3. Sew 5-1/2" x 54-1/2" red orange side borders to opposite sides of the quilt center. Press seams toward the borders. Sew 5-1/2" x 64-1/2" red orange top/bottom borders to the top/bottom of the quilt center to complete the quilt.

Quilt Assembly Diagram

Finishing the Quilt

1. Layer the quilt top, batting and backing. Quilt the layers together.

2. Sew (7) 2-1/4" x wof red orange binding strips together end-to-end. Press the strip in half, wrong sides together, along the length. Sew the binding to the edges of the quilt. Turn binding over the edge to the back and stitch in place.

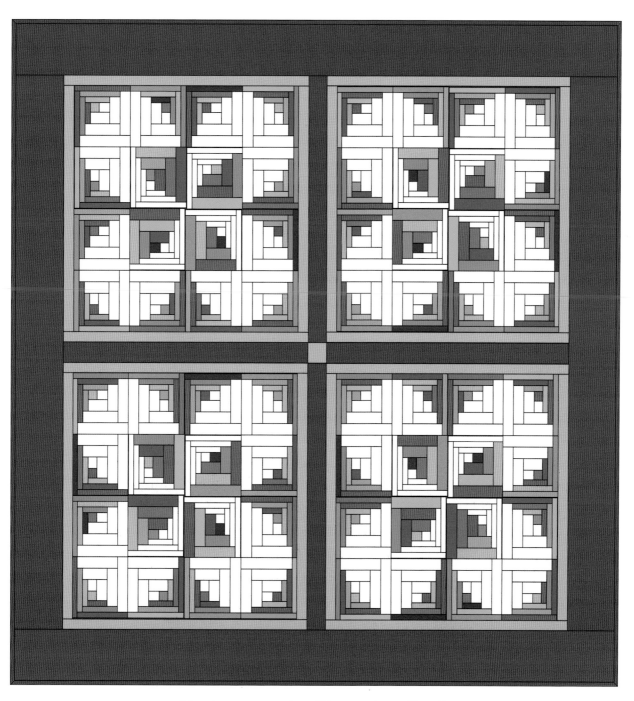

Solomon's Puzzle Quilt
Finished quilt size: 64" x 64"

Dotsy Bed Runner

The curvy log cabin block placement in the bed runner produces star and circle units. Using pre-cut strips makes this a perfect project for a beginner.

Skill level: beginner
Finished bed runner size: 20" x 84"
Curvy log cabin block size: 8" x 8"
20 Block A
wof indicates width of fabric
wofq indicates width of fat quarter

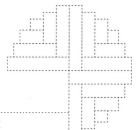

Bed runner designed, pieced and quilted by Jean Ann Wright

Fabric Requirements

- 1 pre-cut bundle of 2-1/2" x wof strips for blocks and binding (You will use 30 strips)
  OR 2-1/8 yards total assorted medium/dark prints cut into (30) 2-1/2" x wof strips

- 1-1/2 yards white fabric for blocks and border

- 2-1/2 yards backing fabric

Cutting

Note: Refer to the Cutting Diagrams for 8" blocks on page 13 to cut the fabric logs to size. The block cutting directions given are for using the Curvy Log Cabin Trim Tool. The trim tool fabric logs must be cut at least 1-1/2" and 2-1/4" wide to allow for trimming.

From white fabric, cut:

(5) 2-1/2" x wof strips for borders.

(20) 1-3/4" squares for block centers.

Cut remaining fabric into
1-1/2" x wof strips for blocks.

Block Assembly

Note: Refer to pages 6-11 to sew the blocks together using your preferred method. Sewing sequence diagrams are provided on pages 12-13 to assist in adding the strips in the correct direction and order.

1. Sew (2) wide medium/dark print strips to adjacent sides of a white center square in a clockwise rotation. Sew (2) narrow white strips to the remaining sides of the center square continuing in a clockwise rotation. This completes round #1. Press the completed round. If you are using the Curvy Log Cabin Trim Tool, trim round #1 to size.

2. Refer to step 1 to add rounds #2 and #3 to the block. Press and trim the logs after each round is complete. Make 20 block A.

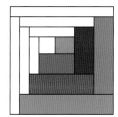

Block A
Make 20

Block Unit Assembly

1. Lay out 4 block A as shown.

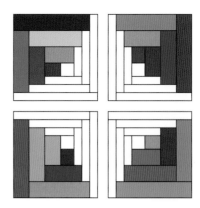

2. Sew the blocks together in rows. Sew the rows together to make a star block unit. Make 3 star block units.

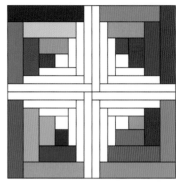

Star block unit
Make 3

3. Lay out 4 block A as shown.

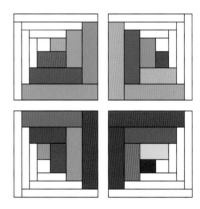

4. Sew the blocks together in rows. Sew the rows together to make a circle block unit. Make 2 circle block units.

Circle block unit
Make 2

Bed Runner Assembly

1. Lay out the 3 star and and 2 circle units as shown in the Runner Assembly Diagram. Sew the units together and press seams to complete the bed runner center.

2. Sew the (5) 2-1/2" x wof white border strips together end-to-end. Press seams open.

3. From the strip cut (2) 2-1/2" x 80-1/2" side borders and (2) 2-1/2" x 20-1/2" top/bottom borders.

4. Sew the side borders to the sides of the bed runner center. Press seams toward the borders.

5. Sew the top/bottom borders to the top and bottom of the bed runner center. Press seams toward borders to complete the bed runner.

Finishing the Bed Runner

1. Layer the bed runner, batting and backing. Quilt the layers together.

2. Sew (6) 2-1/2" x wof pre-cut strips together end-to-end. Press the strip in half, wrong sides together, along the length. Sew the binding to the edges of the quilt. Turn binding over the edge to the back and stitch in place.

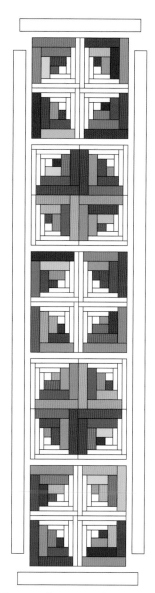

Runner Assembly Diagram

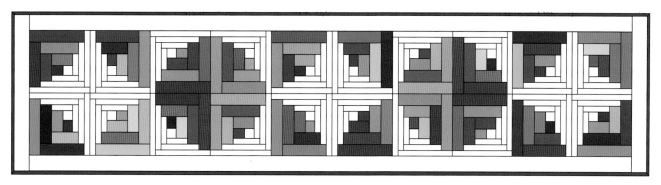

Dotsy Bed Runner
Finished bed runner size: 20" x 84"

Echoes Quilt

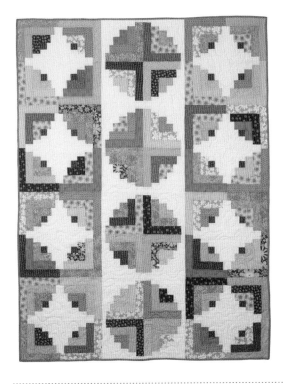

The star and circle units created with the curvy log cabin blocks are lined up in orderly vertical rows in the Echoes Quilt. The bright fabric hues are sewn in a somewhat random manner to create a touch of whimsey.

Skill level: Intermediate
Finished quilt size: 48" x 64"
Curvy log cabin block size: 8" x 8"
16 Block A; 32 Block B
wof indicates width of fabric
wofq indicates width of fat quarter

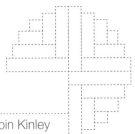

Quilt designed and pieced by Jean Ann Wright; longarm quilted by Robin Kinley

Fabric Requirements

- 1 pre-cut bundle of (40) bright 2-1/2" x wof strips for blocks OR 2-7/8 yards total assorted bright fabrics cut into (40) 2-1/2" x wof strips

- 1 fat quarter each green, pink, lime, yellow, light orange fabrics for blocks

- 2 yards white fabric for blocks

- 1/2 yard green fabric for binding

- 4-1/4 yards backing fabric

Cutting

Note: Refer to the Cutting Diagrams for 8" blocks on page 13 to cut the fabric logs to size. The block cutting directions given are for using the Curvy Log Cabin Trim Tool. The trim tool fabric logs must be cut at least 1-1/2" and 2-1/4" wide to allow for trimming.

From white fabric, cut:

(16) 1-3/4" center squares for block A.

Cut remaining fabric into 1-1/2" x wof strips for blocks A and B.

From pink fat quarter, cut:

(3) 1-3/4" x wofq strips. From the strips cut (32) 1-3/4" center squares for block B.

From assorted fat quarters and remaining pink fat quarter, cut:

2-1/4" x wofq strips for blocks A and B.

From green fabric, cut:

(7) 2-1/4" x wof binding strips.

Block Assembly

Note: Refer to pages 6-11 to sew the blocks together using your preferred method. Sewing sequence diagrams are provided on pages 12-13 to assist in adding the strips in the correct direction and order.

Block A

1. Sew (2) wide bright strips to adjacent sides of a white center square in a clockwise rotation. Sew (2) narrow white strips to the remaining sides of the center square continuing in a clockwise rotation. This completes round #1. Press the completed round. If you are using the Curvy Log Cabin Trim Tool, trim round #1 to size.

2. Refer to step 1 to add rounds #2 and #3 to the block. Press and trim the logs after each round is complete. Make 16 block A.

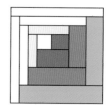

Block A
Make 16

Block B

Note: Each round uses matching wide bright print strips.

1. Sew (2) narrow white strips to adjacent sides of a pink center square in a clockwise rotation. Sew (2) wide bright strips to the remaining sides of the center square continuing in a clockwise rotation. This completes round #1. Press the completed round. If you are using the Curvy Log Cabin Trim Tool, trim round #1 to size.

2. Refer to step 1 to add rounds #2 and #3 to the block. Press and trim the logs after each round is complete. Make 32 block B.

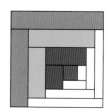

Block B
Make 32

Block Unit Assembly

1. Lay out 4 block A as shown. Sew the blocks together in rows. Sew the rows together to make a circle block unit. Make 4 circle block units.

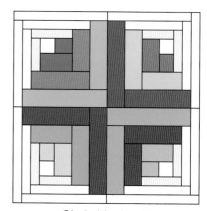

Circle block unit
Make 4

2. Lay out 4 block B as shown. Sew the blocks together in rows. Sew the rows together to make a star block unit. Make 8 star block units.

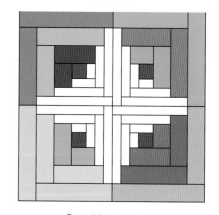

Star block unit
Make 8

Quilt Assembly

1. Lay out the block units in 3 vertical rows as shown. Rows 1 and 3 will each have 4 star block units and row 2 will have 4 circle block units.

2. Sew the block units together in vertical rows. Sew the rows together to complete the quilt top.

Finishing the Quilt

1. Layer the quilt top, batting and backing. Quilt the layers together.

2. Sew (7) 2-1/4" x wof green binding strips together end-to-end. Press the strip in half, wrong sides together, along the length. Sew the binding to the edges of the quilt. Turn binding over the edge to the back and stitch in place.

Echoes Quilt
Finished quilt size: 48" x 64"

Maypole Quilt

Scraps in dramatic red, black and white come together to make this sophisticated quilt design. At first glance it appears challenging, but is actually very easy to sew. Just shuffle the blocks into units to make interesting oval shapes and stack them to create a winding ribbon design.

Skill level: intermediate
Finished quilt size: 50" x 62"
Curvy log cabin block size: 6" x 6"
32 Block A1; 16 Block A2
wof indicates width of fabric
wofq indicates width of fat quarter

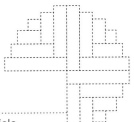

Quilt designed and pieced by Jean Ann Wright; quilted by Alta Miele

Fabric Requirements

- Assorted red print fabric scraps or 16 fat quarters of assorted red prints for blocks
- Assorted black print fabric scraps or 8 fat quarters of assorted black prints for blocks
- 2 yards white fabric for blocks
- Fat quarter white with small black polka dots for blocks
- 1 yard solid black fabric for inner borders, block center squares and binding
- 1-1/3 yards black/white print fabric for outer borders
- 4 yards backing fabric

Cutting

Note: Refer to the Cutting Diagrams for 6" blocks on page 13 to cut the fabric logs to size. The block cutting directions given are for using the Curvy Log Cabin Trim Tool. The trim tool fabric logs must be cut at least 1-1/4" and 1-3/4" wide to allow for trimming.

From assorted red print fabrics, cut:

(32) 1-1/2" center squares for Block A1.

Cut remaining red print fabrics into 1-1/4" x wofq or width of scrap strips for Block A1.

From assorted black print fabrics, cut:

(16) 1-1/2" center squares for Block A2.

Cut remaining black print fabrics into 1-1/4" x wofq or width of scrap strips for Block A2.

From white fabric, cut:

1-3/4" x wof strips for blocks.

From white with small black polka dots fat quarter, cut:

1-3/4" x wofq strips for blocks.

From solid black fabric, cut:

(8) 1-1/2" x wof strips for inner borders. Sew strips together end-to-end and cut:
   (2) 1-1/2" x 48-1/2" side inner border and
   (2) 1-1/2" x 38-1/2" top/bottom inner borders.

(6) 2-1/4" x wof strips for binding.

From black/white print fabric, cut:

(7) 6-1/2" x wof strips. Sew strips together end-to-end, matching the pattern at the seams, and cut:
   (2) 6-1/2" x 70-1/2" side borders and
   (2) 6-1/2" x 58-1/2" top/bottom borders.

Block Assembly

Note: Refer to pages 6-11 to sew the blocks together using your preferred method. Sewing sequence diagrams are provided on pages 12-13 to assist in adding the strips in the correct direction and order.

Block A1
Note: One white with small black polka dots strip was used in each block.

1. Sew (2) wide white strips to adjacent sides of a red print center square in a clockwise rotation. Sew (2) narrow red print strips to the remaining sides of the center square continuing in a clockwise rotation. This completes round #1. Press the completed round. If you are using the Curvy Log Cabin Trim Tool, trim round #1 to size.

2. Refer to step 1 to add rounds #2 and #3 to the block. Press and trim the logs after each round is complete. Make 32 block A1.

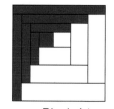

Block A1
Make 32

Block A2
Note: One white with small black polka dots strip was used in each block.

1. Sew (2) wide white strips to adjacent sides of a black print center square in a clockwise rotation. Sew (2) narrow black print strips to the remaining sides of the center square continuing in a clockwise rotation. This completes round #1. Press the completed round. If you are using the Curvy Log Cabin Trim Tool, trim round #1 to size.

2. Refer to step 1 to add rounds #2 and #3 to the block. Press and trim the logs after each round is complete. Make 16 block A2.

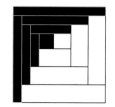

Block A2
Make 16

Block Unit Assembly

1. Lay out 4 block A1 and 2 block A2 as shown. Sew the blocks together in pairs.

2. Sew the pairs together to make a block unit. Make 8 block units.

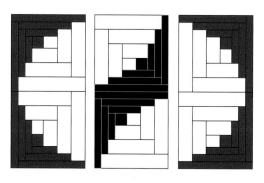

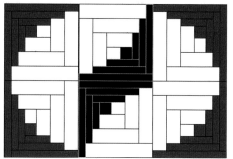

Block unit
Make 8

Quilt Assembly

1. Referring to the Quilt Assembly Diagram, lay out 8 block units in 2 vertical rows with 4 units in each row.

2. Sew the units together in rows. Sew the rows together to complete the quilt center.

3. Sew 1-1/2" x 48-1/2" black side inner borders to opposite sides of the quilt center. Press seams toward the borders. Sew 1-1/2" x 38-1/2" black top/bottom inner borders to the top/bottom of the quilt center. Press seams toward the borders.

4. Fold the 6-1/2" x 70-1/2" black/white print side outer borders in half to find the center. Pin the border strips to opposite sides of the quilt center matching the border and quilt top centers. Center the border design at the center of the quilt. Pin all the way to the outside edges letting any extra fabric at each end remain loose. Repeat with the 6-1/2" x 58-1/2" top/bottom outer border strips.

5. Sew the borders in place starting and stopping 1/4" from the outside edge of the quilt center on each side. Mark a 45-degree angle from the point where the stitching stopped to the outside edge of the border. Repeat on both ends of each border strip.

6. Stitch from the seam line to the outside edge of the border strips on the marked lines. Trim away excess fabric and press seams open to miter the borders.

Finishing the Quilt

1. Layer the quilt top, batting and backing. Quilt the layers together.

2. Sew (6) 2-1/4" x wof solid black binding strips together end-to-end. Press the strip in half, wrong sides together, along the length. Sew the binding to the edges of the quilt. Turn binding over the edge to the back and stitch in place.

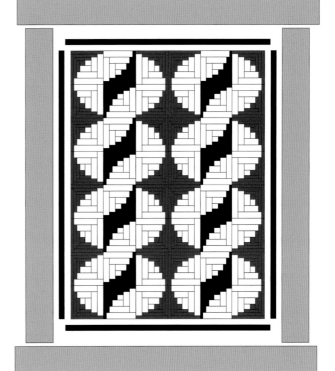

Quilt Assembly Diagram

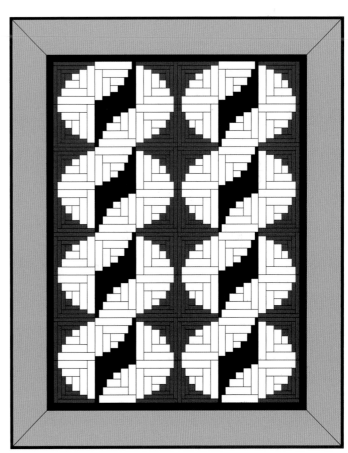

Maypole Quilt
Finished quilt size: 50" x 62"

Ripples Quilt

The Ripples quilt is based on the Barn Raising Log Cabin pattern. A twist here and a turn there create a star center surrounded by ripples of color. A bold border print holds it all together.

Skill level: beginner
Finished quilt size: 62" x 62"
Curvy log cabin block size: 8" x 8"
32 Block A1; 4 Block A2
wof indicates width of fabric
lof indicates length of fabric
wofq indicates width of fat quarter

Quilt designed and pieced by Jean Ann Wright; longarm quilted by Robin Kinley

Fabric Requirements

- 1 fat quarter **each** 12 bright-to-dark print fabrics for blocks
- 1 fat quarter **each** 4 solid fabrics for blocks
- 2 yards ivory fabric for blocks
- 2 yards print fabric for border and binding
- 4-3/4 yards backing fabric

Cutting

Note: Refer to the Cutting Diagrams for 8" blocks on page 13 to cut the fabric logs to size. The block cutting directions given are for using the Curvy Log Cabin Trim Tool. The trim tool fabric logs must be cut at least 1-1/2" and 2-1/4" wide to allow for trimming.

From **each** bright-to-dark print fat quarter, cut:

(1) 1-1/2" x wofq strip for Block A2.

Cut remaining fat quarters into
　　2-1/4" x wofq strips for
　　　Block A1.
　　From one of the dark print
　　strips cut:
　　　(4) 1-3/4" center squares for
　　　　Block A2.

From **each** solid fat quarter, cut:

(1) 1-1/2" x wofq strip for Block A2.

Cut remaining fat quarters into
　　2-1/4" x wofq strips for
　　　Block A1.

From ivory fabric, cut:

(32) 1-3/4" center squares for
　　Block A1.

(8) 2-1/4" x wof strips for Block A2.

Cut remaining fabric into
　　1-1/2" x wof strips for Block A1.

From print fabric, cut:

(4) 7-1/2" x lof strips and cut:
　　(2) 7-1/2" x 48-1/2" side
　　　borders and
　　(2) 7-1/2" x 62-1/2"
　　　top/bottom borders.

(4) 2-1/4" x lof binding strips.

Block Assembly

Note: Refer to pages 6-11 to sew the blocks together using your preferred method. Sewing sequence diagrams are provided on pages 12-13 to assist in adding the strips in the correct direction and order.

Block A1

1. Sew (2) wide bright-to-dark print strips to adjacent sides of an ivory center square in a clockwise rotation. Sew (2) narrow ivory strips to the remaining sides of the center square continuing in a clockwise rotation. This completes round #1. Press the completed round. If you are using the Curvy Log Cabin Trim Tool, trim round #1 to size.

2. Refer to step 1 to add rounds #2 and #3 to the block. Press and trim the logs after each round is complete. Make 32 block A1.

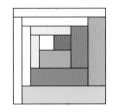

Block A1
Make 32

Block A2

1. Sew (2) narrow bright-to-dark print strips to adjacent sides of a dark print center square in a clockwise rotation. Sew (2) wide ivory strips to the remaining sides of the center square continuing in a clockwise rotation. This completes round #1. Press the completed round. If you are using the Curvy Log Cabin Trim Tool, trim round #1 to size.

2. Refer to step 1 to add rounds #2 and #3 to the block. Press and trim the logs after each round is complete. Make 4 block A2.

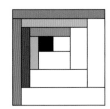

Block A2
Make 4

Block Unit Assembly

1. Lay out 8 block A1 and 1 block A2 in 3 rows as shown.

2. Sew the blocks together in rows. Sew the rows together to make a block unit. Make 4 block units.

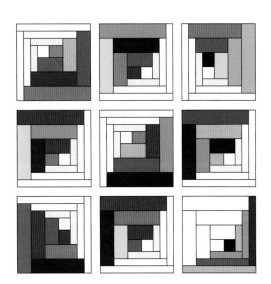

Block unit
Make 4

Quilt Assembly

1. Referring to the Quilt Assembly Diagram, lay out the 4 block units as shown. The 4 block B should form a star in the center of the units.

2. Sew the units together in rows. Sew the rows together to complete the quilt center.

3. Sew 7-1/2" x 48-1/2" print side borders to opposite sides of the quilt center. Press seams toward the borders. Sew 7-1/2" x 62-1/2" print top/bottom borders to the top/bottom of the quilt center to complete the quilt.

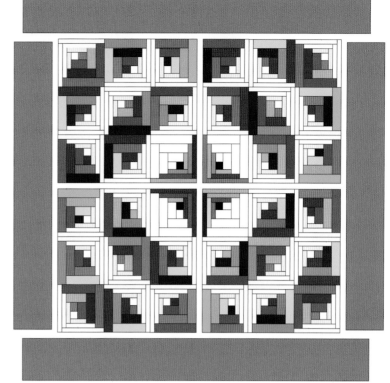

Quilt Assembly Diagram

Finishing the Quilt

1. Layer the quilt top, batting and backing. Quilt the layers together.

2. Sew (4) 2-1/4" x lof print binding strips together end-to-end. Press the strip in half, wrong sides together, along the length. Sew the binding to the edges of the quilt. Turn binding over the edge to the back and stitch in place.

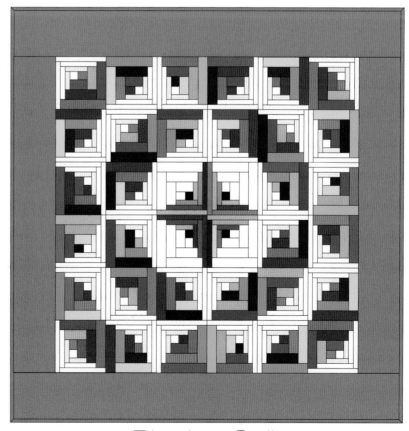

Ripples Quilt
Finished quilt size: 62" x 62"

Bejeweled Quilt

Jewel tone solids are mixed and matched to create the blocks in this cheerful quilt. Blocks featuring bright and light fabrics are stitched into three distinct units to construct the quilt.

Skill level: intermediate

Finished quilt size: 58" x 58"

Curvy log cabin block size: 8" x 8"

24 Block A1; 12 Block A2

wof indicates width of fabric

wofq indicates width of fat quarter

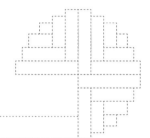

Quilt designed, pieced and quilted by Jean Ann Wright

Fabric Requirements

- 1/3 yard **each** jewel tone fabrics in green, gray, blue, orange, purple, gold and pink for blocks
- 2 yards white fabric for blocks
- 1-3/4 yards orange chevron fabric for borders
- 1/2 yard orange fabric for binding
- 4-3/4 yards backing fabric

Cutting

Note: Refer to the Cutting Diagrams for 8" blocks on page 13 to cut the fabric logs to size. The block cutting directions given are for using the Curvy Log Cabin Trim Tool. The trim tool fabric logs must be cut at least 1-1/2" and 2-1/4" wide to allow for trimming.

From **each** jewel tone fabric, cut:

(3) 2-1/4" x wof strips for Block A2.
    From remaining fabric cut:
    (24) 1-3/4" center squares
        for Block A1.

Cut remaining fabric into
    1-1/2" x wof strips for Block A1.

From white fabric, cut:

(12) 1-3/4" center squares for
    Block A2.

(24) 1-1/2" x wof strips for Block A2.

Cut remaining fabric into
    2-1/4" x wof strips for Block A1.

From orange chevron fabric, fussy cut:

(7) 5-1/2" x wof strips.

Note: You may need to adjust the width of your strips to work with the fabric design.

To fussy cut chevron fabric place a ruler 1/4" from the "V" indentation at the bottom of the strip and 1/4" to peak of chevron on the top of the strip.

From orange fabric, cut:

(7) 2-1/4" x wof binding strips.

Block Assembly

Note: Refer to pages 6-11 to sew the blocks together using your preferred method. Sewing sequence diagrams are provided on pages 12-13 to assist in adding the strips in the correct direction and order.

Block A1

1. Sew (2) wide white strips to adjacent sides of a jewel tone center square in a clockwise rotation. Sew (2) narrow jewel tone strips to the remaining sides of the center square continuing in a clockwise rotation. This completes round #1. Press the completed round. If you are using the Curvy Log Cabin Trim Tool, trim round #1 to size.

2. Refer to step 1 to add rounds #2 and #3 to the block. Press and trim the logs after each round is complete. Make 24 block A1.

Block A1
Make 24

Block A2

1. Sew (2) wide jewel tone strips to adjacent sides of a white center square in a clockwise rotation. Sew (2) narrow white strips to the remaining sides of the center square continuing in a clockwise rotation. This completes round #1. Press the completed round. If you are using the Curvy Log Cabin Trim Tool, trim round #1 to size.

2. Refer to step 1 to add rounds #2 and #3 to the block. Press and trim the logs after each round is complete. Make 12 block A2.

Block A2
Make 12

Bright Star Unit Assembly

Lay out 4 block A1. Sew the blocks together in rows. Sew the rows together to make a bright star unit. Make 4 bright star units.

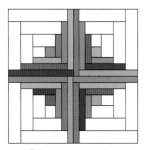

Bright star unit
Make 4

Scallop Unit Assembly

Lay out 2 block A1 and 2 block A2. Sew the blocks together in rows. Sew the rows together to make a scallop unit. Make 4 scallop units.

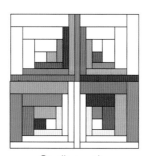

Scallop unit
Make 4

White Star Unit Assembly

Lay out 4 block A2. Sew the blocks together in rows. Sew the rows together to make a white star unit.

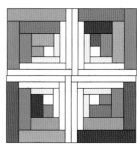

White star unit
Make 1

Quilt Center Assembly

1. Referring to the Quilt Assembly Diagram, lay out the bright star, scallop and white star units in 3 rows with 3 blocks in each row as shown.

2. Sew the units together in rows. Sew the rows together to complete the quilt top.

3. Sew the 5-1/2" x wof orange chevron border strips together end-to-end, carefully matching the chevrons. Press seams open.

4. Cut the strip into (4) 5-1/2" x 70" border strips. Fold each strip in half to find the center. Pin the border strips to each side of the quilt top matching the border and quilt top centers. Pin all the way to the outside edges letting any extra fabric at each end remain loose.

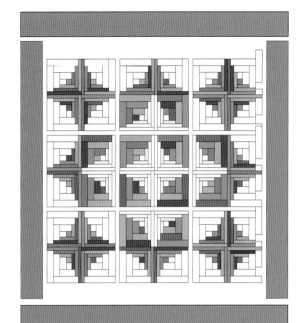

Quilt Assembly Diagram

5. Sew the borders in place starting and stopping 1/4" from the outside edge of the quilt top on each side. Mark a 45-degree angle from the point where the stitching stopped to the outside edge of the border. Repeat on both ends of each border strip.

6. Stitch from the seam line to the outside edge of the border strips on the marked lines. Trim away excess fabric and press seams open to miter the borders.

Finishing the Quilt

1. Layer the quilt top, batting and backing. Quilt the layers together.

2. Sew (7) 2-1/4" x wof orange binding strips together end-to-end. Press the strip in half, wrong sides together, along the length. Sew the binding to the edges of the quilt. Turn binding over the edge to the back and stitch in place.

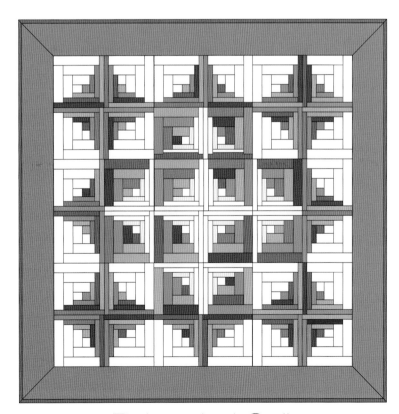

Bejeweled Quilt
Finished quilt size: 58" x 58"

Stringing Beads Quilt

Stringing beads is an entertaining pastime. The curvy log cabin blocks in this quilt resemble fabric beads stitched in rows. Using a wide assortment of prints adds to the fun.

Skill level: beginner
Finished quilt size: 68" x 81"
Curvy log cabin block size: 8" x 8"
56 block A
wof indicates width of fabric
lof indicates length of fabric
wofq indicates width of fat quarter

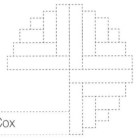

Quilt designed and pieced by Jean Ann Wright; quilted by Jan Cox

Fabric Requirements

- 1 pre-cut bundle of (40) bright and dark print 2-1/2" x wof strips for blocks
  OR 2-7/8 yards total assorted bright and dark print fabrics cut into 2-1/4" x wof strips

Note: The pre-cut 2-1/2" strips will be trimmed to size during the block assembly.

- 1 pre-cut bundle of (42) bright and dark print 10" squares for blocks
  OR 2-3/4 yards total assorted bright and dark print fabrics

- 2 yards assorted white print fabrics for blocks and sashing

- 2 yards light teal print fabric for border and binding

- 5 yards backing fabric

Cutting

Note: Refer to the Cutting Diagrams for 8" blocks on page 13 to cut the fabric logs to size. The block cutting directions given are for using the Curvy Log Cabin Trim Tool. The trim tool fabric logs must be cut at least 1-1/2" and 2-1/4" wide to allow for trimming.

From bright and dark 10" squares, cut:
2-1/4" x wof strips for blocks.

From assorted white print fabrics, cut:
(56) 1-3/4" center squares for blocks.

(8) 1-1/2" x wof strips for sashing. Sew the strips together end-to-end and cut:
  (5) 1-1/2" x 56-1/2" sashing strips.

Cut remaining fabric into 1-1/2" x wof strips for blocks.

From light teal print fabric, cut:
(4) 6-1/2" x lof strips.
  From the strips cut:
    (2) 6-1/2" x 69-1/2" side borders and
    (2) 6-1/2" x 68-1/2" top/bottom borders.

(4) 2-1/4" x lof binding strips.

Block Assembly

Note: Refer to pages 6-11 to sew the blocks together using your preferred method. Sewing sequence diagrams are provided on pages 12-13 to assist in adding the strips in the correct direction and order.

1. Sew (2) wide bright/dark strips to adjacent sides of a white print center square in a clockwise rotation. Sew (2) narrow white print strips to the remaining sides of the center square continuing in a clockwise rotation. This completes round #1. Press the completed round. If you are using the Curvy Log Cabin Trim Tool, trim round #1 to size.

2. Refer to step 1 to add rounds #2 and #3 to the block. Press and trim the logs after each round is complete. Make 56 block A.

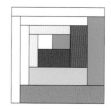

Block A
Make 56

Block Unit Assembly

1. Lay out 2 block A as shown. Sew the blocks together to make a half-circle unit. Make 4 half-circle units.

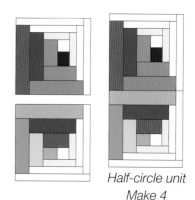

Half-circle unit
Make 4

2. Lay out 4 block A as shown.

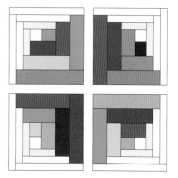

3. Sew the blocks together in rows. Sew the rows together to make a circle unit. Make 12 circle units.

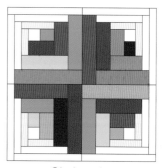

Circle unit
Make 12

Quilt Assembly

1. Lay out the circle and half-circle units in 4 rows with 4 units in each row as shown in the Quilt Assembly Diagram.

2. Sew the units together in rows.

3. Referring to the Quilt Assembly Diagram, sew a 1-1/2" x 56-1/2" white print sashing strip to the top of each row and the bottom of the bottom row.

4. Sew the rows together to complete the quilt center.

5. Sew 6-1/2" x 69-1/2" light teal print side borders to opposite sides of the quilt center. Press seams toward the borders. Sew 6-1/2" x 68-1/2" light teal print top/bottom borders to the top/bottom of the quilt center to complete the quilt.

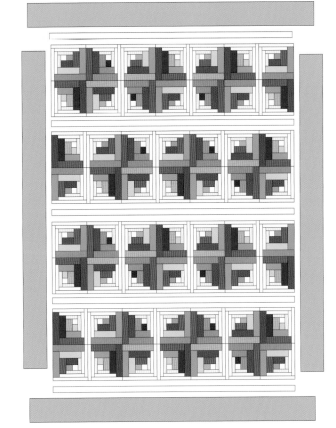

Quilt Assembly Diagram

Finishing the Quilt

1. Layer the quilt top, batting and backing. Quilt the layers together.

2. Sew (4) 2-1/4" x lof light teal print binding strips together end-to-end. Press the strip in half, wrong sides together, along the length. Sew the binding to the edges of the quilt. Turn binding over the edge to the back and stitch in place.

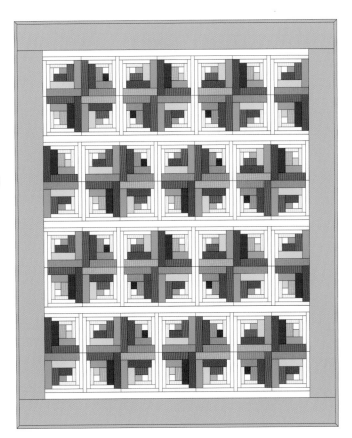

Stringing Beads Quilt
Finished quilt size: 68" x 81"

Paisley Table Runner

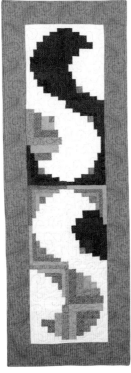

The Paisley Table Runner offers a new twist on the traditional log cabin block. The light/dark strips that make up the block design have been moved around within each block to create a new placement. Create your own designs by playing around with ideas using paper and colored pencils or a computer drawing program.

Skill level: experienced
Finished table runner size: 18" x 54"
Curvy log cabin block size: 6" x 6"
16 blocks
wof indicates width of fabric
wofq indicates width of fat quarter

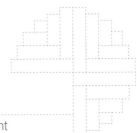

Table runner designed, pieced and quilted by Jean Ann Wright

Fabric Requirements

- 3 fat quarters in assorted black prints for blocks

- 3 fat quarters in assorted aqua prints for blocks

- 1 yard light beige print fabric for center squares and blocks

- 3/4 yard rust paisley print fabric for center squares, border and binding

- 1 yard backing fabric

Cutting

Note: Refer to the Cutting Diagrams for 6" blocks on page 13 to cut the fabric logs to size. The block cutting directions given are for using the Curvy Log Cabin Trim Tool. The trim tool fabric logs must be cut at least 1-1/4" and 1-3/4" wide to allow for trimming.

From each assorted black print fat quarters, cut:

(5) 1-3/4" x wofq strips for blocks.

(5) 1-1/4" x wofq strips for blocks.

From each assorted aqua print fat quarters, cut:

(5) 1-3/4" x wofq strips for blocks.

(5) 1-1/4" x wofq strips for blocks.

From light beige print fabric, cut:

(6) 1-1/2" center squares for blocks.

(6) 1-3/4" x wof strips for blocks.

(12) 1-1/4" x wof strips for blocks.

From rust paisley print fabric, cut:

(10) 1-1/2" center squares for blocks.

(3) 3-1/2" x wof strips for borders. Sew the strips together end-to-end and cut:
    (2) 3-1/2" x 48-1/2" side border strips and
    (2) 3-1/2" x 18-1/2" top/bottom border strips.

(5) 2-1/4" x wof binding strips.

From backing fabric, cut:

(2) 22" x 36" pieces. Sew the pieces together along the 22" ends and press seam open.

Block Assembly

Note: Refer to pages 6-11 to sew the blocks together using your preferred method.

1. Sew (2) wide light beige print strips to adjacent sides of a rust paisley center square in a clockwise rotation. Sew (2) narrow assorted black print strips to the remaining sides of the center square continuing in a clockwise rotation. This completes round #1. Press the completed round. If you are using the Curvy Log Cabin Trim Tool, trim round #1 to size.

2. Refer to step 1 to add rounds #2 and #3 to the block. Press and trim the logs after each round is complete. Make 3 blocks.

Make 3

3. Referring to steps 1 – 2 and the diagrams, make the remaining blocks in the same manner. Make a total of 16 blocks.

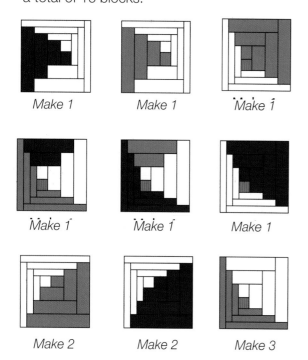

Make 1	Make 1	Make 1
Make 1	Make 1	Make 1
Make 2	Make 2	Make 3

Table Runner Assembly

1. Using a flat surface or design wall, lay out the blocks in 8 rows with 2 blocks in each row as shown in the Row Assembly Diagram.

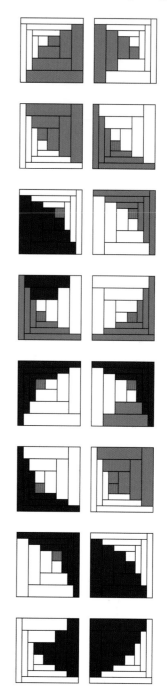

Row Assembly Diagram

2. Sew the blocks in each row together, carefully watching the orientation of the blocks in each row.

3. Check the block placement again and sew the rows together to complete the table runner center.

4. Sew 3-1/2" x 48-1/2" rust paisley print side borders to opposite sides of the table runner center. Press seams toward the borders. Sew 3-1/2" x 18-1/2" rust paisley print top/bottom borders to the top/bottom of the table runner center to complete the table runner.

Finishing the Table Runner

1. Layer the table runner top, batting and backing. Quilt the layers together.

2. Sew (5) 2-1/4" x wof rust paisley print binding strips together end-to-end. Press the strip in half, wrong sides together, along the length. Sew the binding to the edges of the runner. Turn binding over the edge to the back and stitch in place.

Paisley Table Runner
Finished table runner size: 18" x 54"

Resources

Andover Fabrics™
www.andoverfabrics.com

Checker Distributors®
Curvy Log Cabin Trim Tool for retail shops
available exclusively from Checker Distributors
www.checkerdist.com

Creative Grids® USA
Youtube Video –
    "How to Use the Curvy Log
    Cabin Trim Tool"
http://www.youtube.com
    watch?v=FEJrvyaniJk

Curvy Log Cabin Trim Tool for online shopping
www.jeanannquilts.com

Jean Ann Wright's website and blog
www.jeanannquilts.com
www.jeanannquilts.blogspot.com

Landauer Publishing
www.landauerpub.com

Moda Fabrics
www.unitednotions.com

Riley Blake Designs
www.rileyblakedesigns.com

About the Author

Jean Ann Wright has been sewing and making quilts for over 25 years. She majored in textiles and fine arts at Palm Beach State College and has combined these two disciplines to become a fiber artist. From 1986 to 2006 she edited an international quilting magazine titled *QUILT*, plus a variety of special interest quilting titles with the same publishing company.

Jean Ann is the co-author of *Circle of Nine, Log Cabin Quilts: The Basics & Beyond, Quilting a Circle of Nine* and *The Best of Circle of Nine*. She is the author of *Quilt Sashings & Settings: The Basics & Beyond, Jelly Roll Jambalaya* and is the designer of several specialty rulers from Creative Grids®.